Bible Phonics
Workbook 2

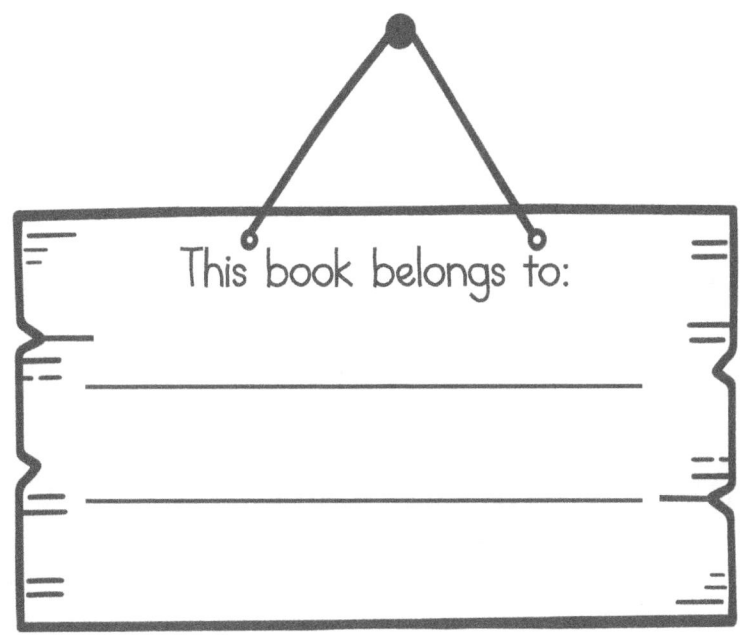
This book belongs to:

Quail Publishers

About the Series

Quail Publishers' Bible Phonics series is a revised version of the Success with Phonics series. The series includes comprehensive, high quality, Bible-based products that are aligned to English language K-2 standards. The program utilizes the Science of Reading components: phonemic awareness, phonics, vocabulary, fluency, and comprehension to ensure literacy. The explicit, systematic phonics strategies get children reading and writing from an early age, while promoting Bible principles and teachings. Each book covers a group of the most common sound-spelling combinations of the English language, with engaging, multi-sensory activities for children to read fluently and confidently.

Quail Publishers

Quail Publishers grants teachers permission to photocopy the designated reproducible pages from this book for classroom use. No other part of this publication may be reproduced, stored in a retrieval system or transmitted in any form or by any means, electronic, mechanical, photocopying, recording or otherwise, without the prior permission of the publisher.

Written by Allison Hall
Interior design by Allison Hall
Bible Illustrations by Wayne Powell
Other illustrations sourced from Pixabay, Dreamstime and FreePik. Used under license.
Bible verses adapted from the Authorized King James Version
Text Copyright © 2023 by Allison Hall
All rights reserved. Published by Quail Publishers LLC
Coral Springs, Florida USA
Email: info@quailpublishers.com or quailpublishers@gmail.com
Website: www.quailpublishers.com

ISBN: 978-0-9894627-8-5

Table of Contents

Introduction	4
Reviewing Sounds and Common Words	9
The /E/ sound	10
The /U/ sound	12
The /R/ sound	14
The /H/ sound	16
High Frequency Words (the)	18
Blending, Spelling Reading	19
High Frequency Words (to)	20
The /B/ sound	21
The /F/ sound	23
High Frequency Words (of, his, has)	26
The /L/ sound	25
The /S/ sound (ss)	34
Blending, Spelling Reading	35
High Frequency Words (go, no, so)	34
Reviewing Sounds	37
Rhymes	38
Building Words, Word Families	39
Steps to Spelling	40
The Alphabet	41
Picture Clues, Nursery Rhyme	42
Comprehension	43
Building Sentences	44
Reading	45
Syllabication	46
Colors and their names	47
Word List	48

Introduction

Bible Phonics™ is an engaging, explicit and systematic approach to teach phonics, integrated with Bible teachings, concepts, and themes. In Bible Phonics™ A-B-C, the first book in the series, children were taught alphabetic recognition skills. However, in the second series of Bible Phonics™ workbooks, the letters are not taught in alphabetic order. The letters, **s**, **a**, **t**, and **p**, are introduced first. This phoneme sequence is used in many English-speaking countries, as it allows children to build and read words quickly and easily. Using this sequence, children can build the words: **at**, **sat**, **pat**, **tap** and **sap**, with the first four letters. Each letter is introduced with a connected Bible story to foster Bible knowledge and as reinforcement. High frequency words with irregular spelling patterns are also taught, using the **Read-Spell-Write** strategy.

TEACHING WITH THE ACTIVITY SHEETS

Bible Phonics™ is suitable for Christian schools, churches and homes. The workbooks fully complement the kindergarten and children's Bible class curriculums. There are two reproducible pages dedicated to teaching each letter sound and its connected Bible lesson. There are also activities to help you review the sounds taught. When children participate in the multisensory activities in the books, they learn:

- **Bible Teachings:** Learn about Christ's teachings, life in ancient Israel and more
- **Phonemic Awareness**: Identify sounds in spoken words
- **Phonics:** Understand letter-sound correspondences
- **Handwriting**: Write the letters and letter combinations that represent each sound
- **Spelling**:
    * Use picture clues to complete words with the target sound
    * Identify the correct spelling of words with the target sound
- **Reading**: Read decodable sentences with words with the target sound
- **Composition:** Build sentences with the target sound
- **Comprehension**: Read decodable stories and rhymes

The pace of each lesson is always dependent on children's mastery of each letter sound and understanding of the lesson. Children should also fully understand a letter sound, before another is introduced.

Using the Bible to teach the Phonics
Before the Lesson

1. Review all aspects of the letter and main picture you will be teaching.

2. Read the Bible story, or connected text, and further literature on phonics.

3. Develop an exciting and engaging lesson which allows for multisensory activities and integrate technology, where applicable.

4. Make sure that children have the necessary stationery and resources to participate in the lesson.

5. Ensure lessons have activities to foster home-school connections.

6. Be aware that some children will have more advanced phonics knowledge than others. Use differentiated instruction to meet each student's needs.

Teaching the Lesson

7a. **Sound Review** – Review previously taught sounds and high frequency words with irregular spelling.

7b. **Phonemic Awareness – Invite children to listen carefully as you say the sound you are teaching. Precise pronunciation, or pure sounds should be said for all letters.** Slide the sound into the picture name. For example say, /ffffish/. Always, stress the sound you are teaching and model the proper mouth position to say each letter sound correctly. Ask children to repeat the sound thrice. Invite them to name the letter that says the sound.

Note that some sounds are continuous and can be easily stretched (stretchy sounds), for example /f/. However some are non-continuous sounds and can't be stretched (bouncy sounds), for example /ĕ/. Non-continuous sounds must be said at least thrice, so that children hear them clearly. Children should also be made aware that a sound can be represented by two letters, for example 'ch' stands for /ch/. This is called a digraph, however in a consonant blend such as c/l, both sounds are heard. Children should be taught to sound out the digraph, not the sounds of the individual letters.

8. **Phonics - Inform children that every letter has a name and a shape, and stands for a sound, or sounds. For example, letter 'e' stands for /ĕ/, as in egg. Draw their attention to the supporting main picture in their workbooks.** If there is a child in the class with a name that begins with the letter and sound you are teaching, say his/her name. For example say, "/ĕ/ is also for Eric". Briefly discuss aspects of the main picture. For example inform children that we use eggs to make many dishes, and the life cycle of many animals start from eggs.

9. **Letter Formation - Write the letter in its upper and lower case forms on the board.** Show the sequence in which each letter is formed and the proper pencil grip. Have children use the activity sheets to write the letters properly, and develop beautiful and legible hand writing.

Use mnemonics where necessary. For example, for lower-case 'f', you can say, "Make it look like a candy cane. Curve slightly left, then go down in a straight line. Draw a flat line across your first line". Point out to children that letters look alike and have various shapes or font styles. For example: 'b' and 'd' are often confused.

10. **Letter Knowledge - Inform children that letter sounds can be heard at the beginning, middle and end of words.** The activities in the book allow children to further build their letter knowledge. Always read and explain the instructions to children.

11. **Reading Connection - Read the Bible story relating to each main picture to promote reading, Bible knowledge,** a sense of story, comprehension skills, and as reinforcement strategies. Ask students questions about each story. There are also sentences and short passages that children must read to apply, practice and master their phonics skills. Students should also be engaged in other interesting multicultural literature daily.

12. **Blending – As soon as children have learned the first three letters, they should be taught to blend letter sounds to read words with vowel-consonant (VC), and consonant-vowel-consonant (CVC) phonemes.** These are popularly called green words, as they are phonetically decodable. The green symbolizes 'go,' as children should read them easily. Use onsets and rimes (word families) to help children to read and spell these words quickly.

13. **Writing – Once children have learned a number of words, you should guide them in spelling, reading, and composing simple sentences.** Reinforce that a sentence starts with a capital letter and has an end mark.

14. **Reinforcement – Use songs, puppets, art and craft, and other activities to make the lessons more engaging and meaningful, integrate subject areas, and reinforce the letter and sound being taught.** Revise the letters of alphabet in sequence often.

15. **Assessment** – Use authentic assessment tools to measure students' progress.

Blending Words

Blending is a very important phonics skill that children must master to read words and build fluency. Blending is the first stage in reading as letters are no longer seen in isolation. It involves sliding the individual speech sounds (phonemes) in a word quickly, in order to decode the word. Mastery of blending words improves with modeling and practice. Always model the blending process and reinforce the procedures. Here are some steps to take when blending a word.

1. Write the word '**at**' on the board. Place sound buttons or dots (•) under the letters in the words. Sound buttons tell children how many phonemes are in a word. To indicate a digraph or trigraph, a line is used.
2. Point to the letter '**a**' and invite the children to say its sound. Then point to letter '**t**' and invite the children to say its sound.
3. Sound talk the word while slowly sliding your finger under it. Sound talk is saying the sounds in the word slowly, only leaving a short gap between words. Say, **a→t**.
4. Do the procedure again quickly and say the word /**at**/. Avoid pausing between sounds. Invite students to say the word. Ask them how many sounds are in the word. Always explain the meaning of unfamiliar words.
5. Add the letter '**s**' at the beginning of the word and invite children to say the new word. Place new words on the word wall. Then inform children to place it in their word bank.
6. Provide opportunities for children to work as partners to spell green words, using onsets and rimes (word families). This can be done with letter cards or tiles.

High Frequency Words

High frequency words are those words that appear most frequently in texts. These words include, '**and**', '**I**', '**is**', '**the**', '**can**' and '**to**'. Children must learn these words very early in order to read sentences automatically, accurately and fluently. Some high frequency words can be decoded easily, as they follow the regular spelling rules. However, some have tricky parts that do not follow the regular spelling rules and can be a challenge for young readers. These irregular spelled words are called sight words or tricky words or red words, as it is expected that children should *read them when they see them*. There are also some words, such as '**her**' and '**like**', that do not have an irregular spelling pattern. However, they can be taught as sight words, as children may not yet be introduced to their sounds and spellings.

Teaching Sight Words

The Bible Phonics™ program uses the Read-Write-Spell strategy to teach sight or tricky words. Here some steps to teach sight words using this strategy.

- Say the sight word being taught three times. Ask children to repeat the word twice.

- Invite children to sound out the letters in the word.

- Discuss the irregular, or tricky part of the word (*where the letter does not correspond to the sound, or sounds children associate with that letter*). For example, letter 's' <u>can</u> stand for /z/ in words.

- Have children trace the word, after which they will spell the word on their own.

- Write the sight word on a card and place it on a word wall. Color-code the word, to remind children of the tricky part. Children should write it in their word bank.

- Refer to the word regularly until children learn it.

Reinforcement Strategies

Word Wall
A word wall is a great tool that supports phonics instruction. It is a display of words, or word parts, that is used to teach spelling, reading and writing. Mount words with the sound-spelling being taught or sight words on a wall as reinforcement.

Word Bank
A word bank is a great way for children to improve their vocabulary, create a word list, reinforce alphabetical order and memorize the spelling of unfamiliar words. Children may use a notebook to create their word banks. Have them devote a sheet of paper for each letter. At the top of each page, they should write each letter in its upper and lower-case forms. Ensure that they start with letters '**Aa**', as the bank should be arranged in alphabetical order. Children should place new words they have learned in their bank.

Name _____   Date _____

Reviewing Sounds and Common Words

These are some common words with the letter sounds that you learned in workbook 1. Say the sounds. Read the words below.

s a t p i n

m d g o c k

it is in am at

an on sit sat

can not dad

did mom cot

nap dog cat

man map pig

and sick pack

Name _____   Date _____

The /ĕ/ Sound

Say the picture name. Listen for **first** sound. Say the sound. It is the short 'e' sound.

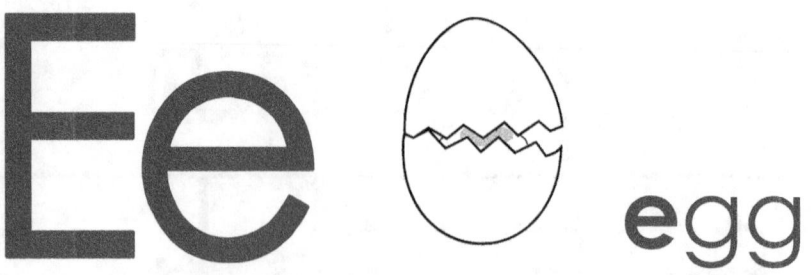

Story Time: Listen carefully as your teacher, or parent, reads the Bible story below. What did you learn from the story?

Bible Story: Enjoy Eggs
Bible Lesson: Deuteronomy 22:6-7
Bible Theme: Care for Others

Do you eat eggs? Many people do. Some people boil or fry their eggs. Others decorate them or use them in pastries. Eggs are also used in juices and as medicine.

Babies come from eggs. It is the first stage in the life cycle of most animals.

Some animals such as dogs, come from eggs that are inside their mothers' bodies. Other animals such as birds, come from eggs that are kept outside of their mothers' bodies.

Birds lay their eggs in nests. They then sit on them to keep them warm. They do this until they hatch into chicks.

The Bible says that we should not take the mother and all her eggs or chicks from a nest. We must never take more than we need. In this way, we show that we care for others, even animals. **We must always care for all living things.**

Name _____   Date _____

Handwriting
Trace and write.

Spelling
Say the name of each picture. Then write the missing letters to complete the words.

___ggplant   h___n   b___d

Identifying Sounds
Say the name of each picture. Then circle those that **begin** with the sound /ĕ/.

 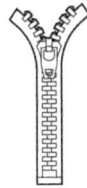 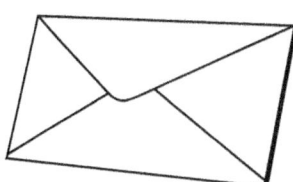

Name _____   Date _____

The /ŭ/ Sound

Say the picture name. Listen for the **first** sound. Say the sound. It is the short 'u' sound.

Uzzah

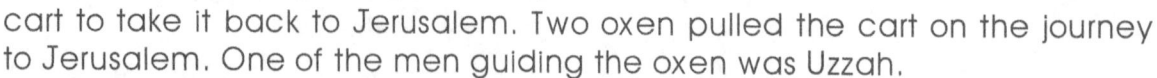

Story Time: Listen carefully as your teacher, or parent, reads the Bible story below. What did you learn from the story?

Bible Story: Uzzah and the Ark
Bible Lesson: 2 Samuel 6:1-7
Bible Theme: Obey God

The Ark of the Covenant was a special box where Israel's holy objects were kept. Two of these objects were a pair of stone tablets. The ten main laws, or the Ten Commandments, were written on these two tablets.

King David wanted to move the Ark to Jerusalem. One day some men put the Ark on a new cart to take it back to Jerusalem. Two oxen pulled the cart on the journey to Jerusalem. One of the men guiding the oxen was Uzzah.

The Israelites were very happy that the Ark was going to Jerusalem. They played music and danced. However, one of the oxen slipped. Uzzah did not want the Ark to fall. He put out his hand and touched the Ark. God was upset and struck Uzzah. Only special people should carry, or touch the Ark.

God struck Uzzah because he was disobedient. **We must always obey God.**

Name _____ Date _____

Handwriting
Trace and write.

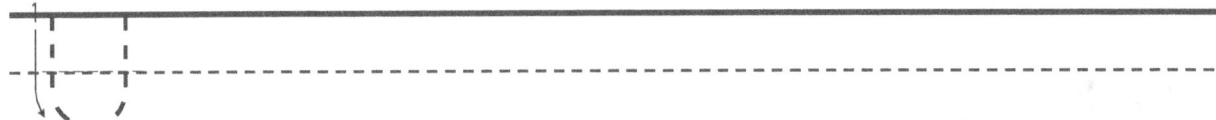

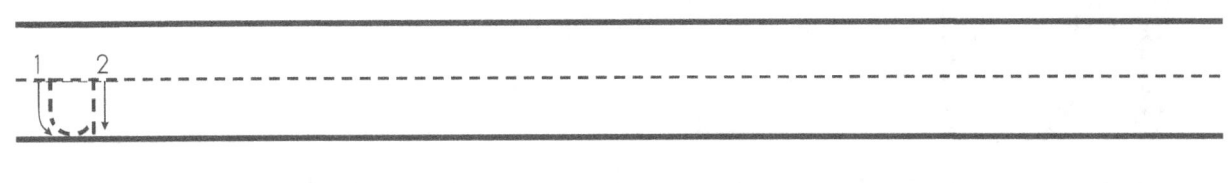

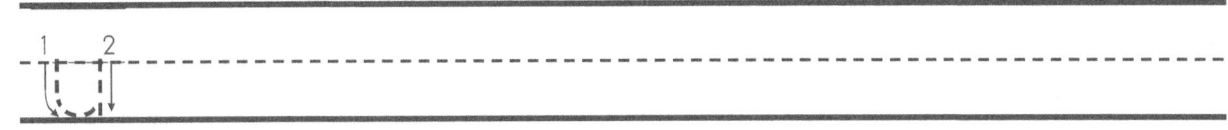

Spelling
Say the name of each picture. Then write the missing letters to complete the words.

___nderpants   dr___m   s___n

Identifying Sounds
Say the name of each picture. Then circle those that **begin** with the sound /ŭ/.

Name _____ Date _____

The /r/ Sound

Say the picture name. Listen for the **first** sound. Say the sound.

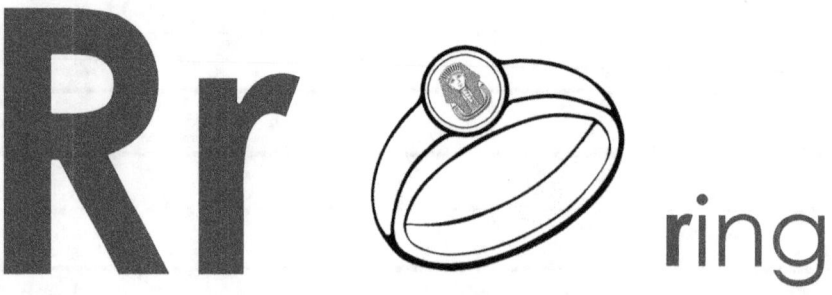

Rr ring

Story Time: Listen carefully as your teacher, or parent, reads the Bible story below. What did you learn from the story?

Bible Story: Royal Ring for Joseph
Bible Lesson: Genesis 41:1-43
Bible Theme: God Gives Wisdom

Joseph was a prisoner in Egypt. A wicked woman had told a lie on him. Her husband believed and put Joseph in prison. While Joseph was in prison, Pharaoh, the king, had two dreams. None of the wise men in the land could tell Pharaoh the meaning of his dreams.

A cupbearer remembered that Joseph had told him about his dreams. He quickly told Pharaoh about Joseph. Pharaoh sent for Joseph. Joseph told the king the meaning of his dreams. Pharaoh was very happy.

"God has shown you this Joseph," he said. "There is no one as wise. You will now be my prime minister."

Joseph rose from a prisoner to a prime minister. Pharoah gave him a ring for royals. He gave him expensive clothes and put a gold chain around his neck. Later, Pharaoh told Joseph to bring his family to Egypt to live.

It was God who made Joseph wise. **God gives wisdom to those who obey him.**

Name _____ Date _____

Handwriting
Trace and write.

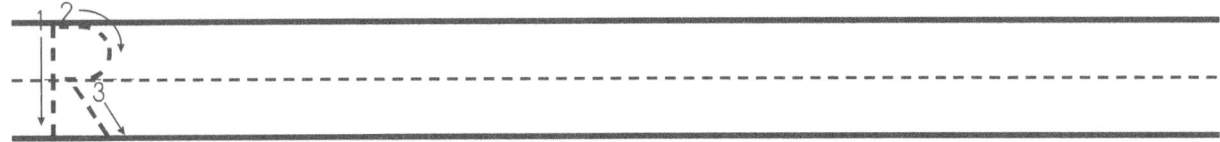

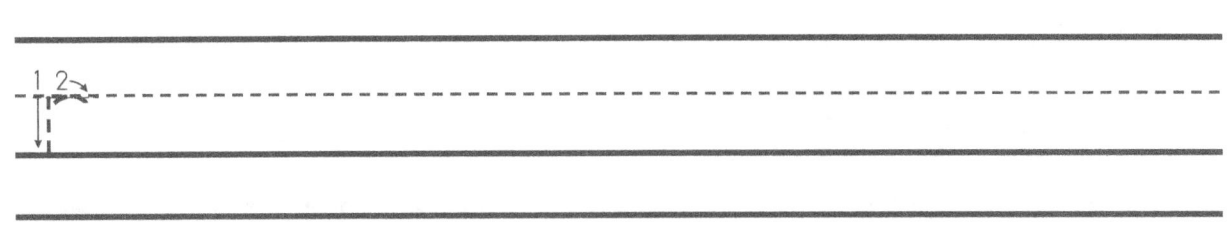

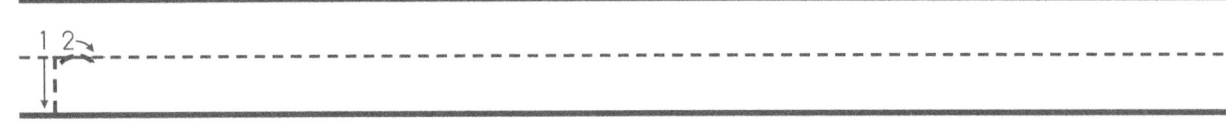

Spelling
Say the name of each picture. Then write the missing letters to complete the words.

___abbit   ___at   pi___ate

Identifying Sounds
Say the name of each picture. Then circle those that **begin** with the sound /r/.

      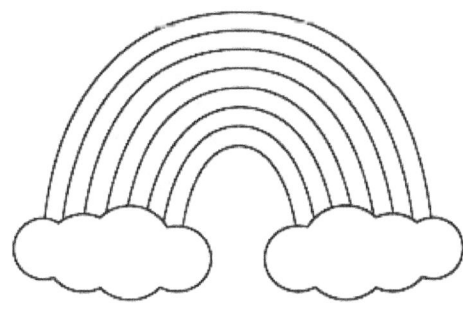

Name _____   Date _____

The /h/ Sound

Say the picture name. Listen for the **first** sound. Say the sound.

Hh harp

Story Time: Listen carefully as your teacher, or parent, reads the Bible story below. What did you learn from the story?

Bible Story: The Harp that Heals
Bible Lesson: 1 Samuel 16:14-23
Bible Theme: Be Happy

One day King Saul of Israel was feeling very sad. This feeling was lasting very long. The servants were very worried about him.

One of them said, "Let us see if an evil spirit is hurting you. Give the order for us to find a man who plays the harp well. When he plays the harp, you will feel better."

So King Saul said to his servants, "Find someone who plays the harp well and bring him to me." One of the servants told the king about David.

David was a shepherd boy and musician. He played the harp very well.

King Saul sent his messengers to Jesse, David's father. He asked Jesse to send David to play for him. Jesse sent David to play for King Saul. The king was very happy to meet David. When he felt sad, David played his harp to calm him and make him happy.

God wants us to be happy so that we can worship him freely.

Name _____   Date _____

Handwriting
Trace and write.

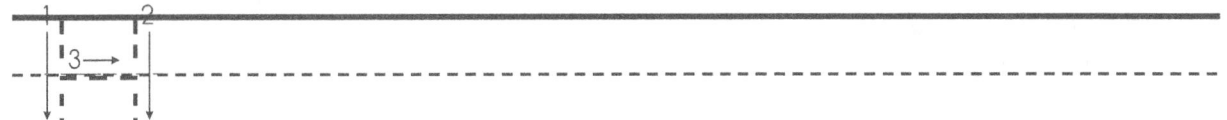

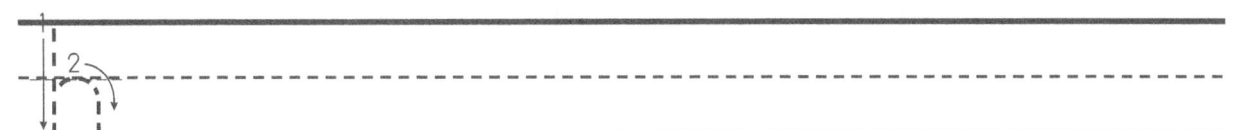

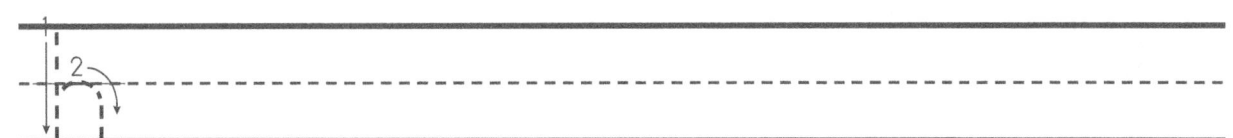

Spelling
Say the name of each picture. Then write the missing letters to complete the words.

____en   ____ouse   ____elicopter

Identifying Sounds
Say the name of each picture. Then circle those that **begin** with the sound /h/.

Name _____   Date _____

 High Frequency Word

Read
Say the word.

Write
Write the word.

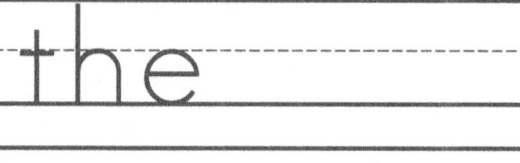

Spell
Circle the correct spelling of the word.

the   he   the   thee

Trace the word '**the**' to complete the sentence. Read the sentence.

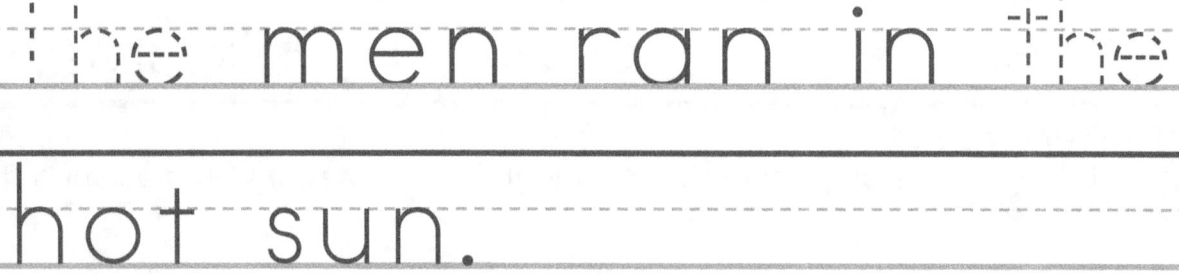

Color the word. Then write it in your word bank book.

Name _____   Date _____

Blending
Use sound talk to say the letter sounds in each word. Then blend the sounds to read the words.

s u n   p e n   c u p

m u d   r u n   h e n

Spelling
Say the picture names. Then circle the correct spelling for each picture.

hut   hat   pen   den   sun   run

Reading
Read the sentence based on Genesis 44:1-34.

The man hid a cup in the sack.

Name _____   Date _____

 High Frequency Word

Read
Say the word.

Write
Write the word.

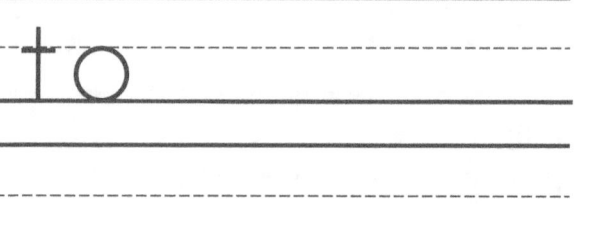

Spell
Circle the correct spelling of the word.

to   too   the   to

Trace the word 'to' to complete the sentence. Read the sentence.

Color the word. Then write it in your word bank book.

Name _____   Date _____

The /b/ Sound

Say the picture name. Listen for the **first** sound. Say the sound.

Bb

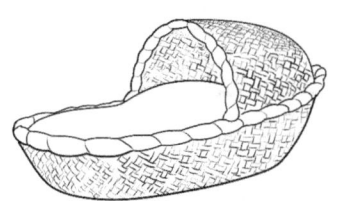

basket

Story Time: Listen carefully as your teacher, or parent, reads the Bible story below. What did you learn from the story?

> **Bible Story**: A Baby in a Basket
> **Bible Lesson**: Exodus 2:1-10
> **Bible Theme**: God Saves

Pharaoh the King of Egypt did not like the Hebrews. He felt there were too many of them in Egypt. One day he said that all Hebrew baby boys should be thrown into River Nile.

A Hebrew woman had a baby boy. She did not want the baby to be killed, so she hid him. The baby was growing up fast. The mother could not hide the baby any longer. She made a basket and rubbed it with tar. The mother put the baby in the basket, then laid it by the river bank. The baby's sister hid in the bushes and watched over him.

Pharaoh's daughter soon came to the river. She saw the basket and asked her servants to get it. When she opened it, she saw the baby.

"This is a Hebrew baby!" Pharaoh's daughter said. The baby's sister quickly came and said, "Shall I get a Hebrew woman to nurse the baby for you?" Pharaoh's daughter said yes, and the baby's sister got her mother.

The mother was glad that her baby was not killed. Pharaoh's daughter took the baby as her son. She named the baby Moses because she took him out of the water. It was God who caused the baby to be saved. **God saves us in times of trouble.**

Name _____   Date _____

Handwriting
Trace and write.

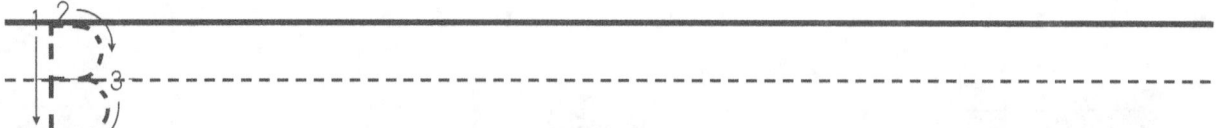

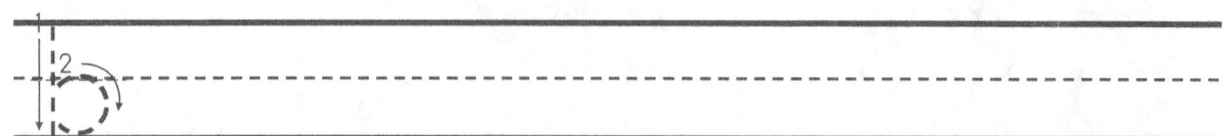

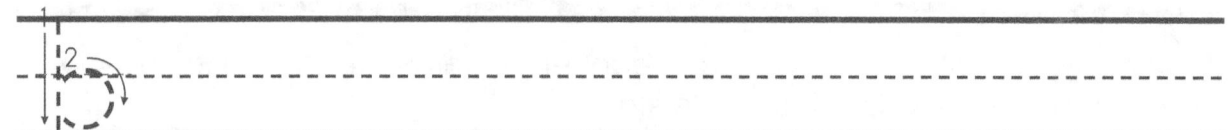

Spelling
Say the name of each picture. Then write the missing letters to complete the words.

___oat   ta___let   cra___

Identifying Sounds
Say the name of each picture. Then circle those that **begin** with the sound /b/.

The /f/ Sound

Say the picture name. Listen for the **first** sound. Say the sound.

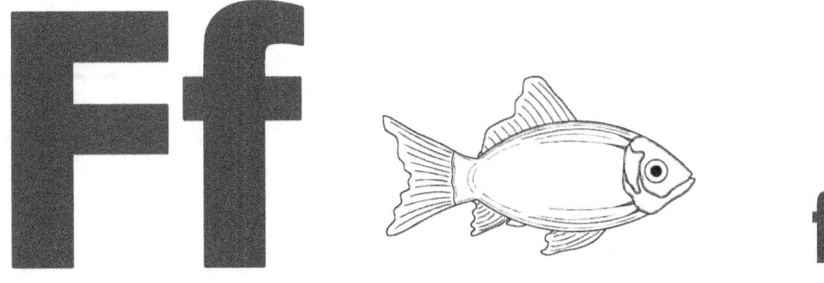

Ff   fish

Story Time: Listen carefully as your teacher, or parent, reads the Bible story below. What did you learn from the story?

Bible Story: Food for Friends
Bible Lesson: John 6:1-13
Bible Theme: God Provides

One day a large crowd kept following Jesus. They followed him because of the many good things he did. Jesus went by the mountainside and sat down beside his disciples. It was late, and the people were tired and hungry.

Jesus said to Phillip, "Where will we get food for all these people?" Jesus said this just to test Phillip. He knew what he was going to do.

Andrew found a little boy who had food. The boy had five loaves of bread and two fish. He thought it was not enough for so many people. But Jesus took the food and thanked God for it. He broke the food into many pieces and gave it to his disciples. They gave the food to the hungry people. That day, Jesus shared the food with five thousand people. It was indeed a miracle! The people were so happy that Jesus had provided for them. They ate and ate. Soon, they were all full. When the disciples gathered what was left over, it filled twelve baskets. **God always provides for his people.**

Name _____   Date _____

Handwriting
Trace and write.

Spelling
Say the name of each picture. Then write the missing letters to complete the words.

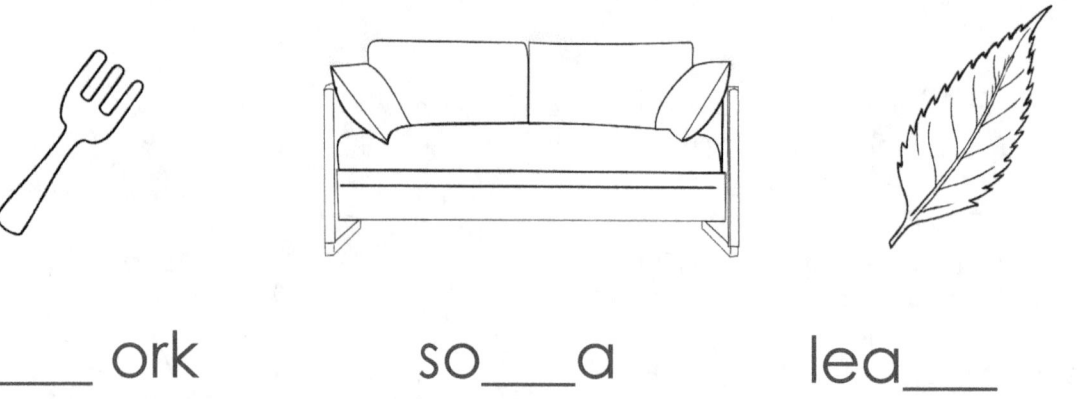

___ ork   so___a   lea___

Identifying Sounds
Say the name of each picture. Then circle those that **begin** with the sound /f/.

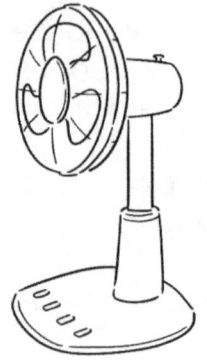 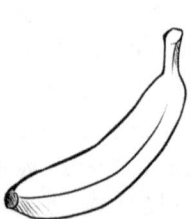 

Name _____   Date _____

The /f/ Sound

Say the picture name. Listen for the **last** sound. Say the sound. The letters '**ff**' stand for one sound, /f/ as in cliff.

cliff

Phonics Tip: When the sound /f/ is heard after a short vowel sound in a one-syllable word, it is usually spelled with the letters '**ff**'. For example: cliff.

Blending
Use sound talk to say the letter sounds in each word. Then blend the sounds to read the words. How many sounds are in each word?

off   puff   cuff

Reading
Read the caption based on, The Wise and Foolish Builders, Matthew 27:24-27.

Huff and puff!

Name _____   Date _____

 High Frequency Word

Read
Say the word.

Write
Write the word.

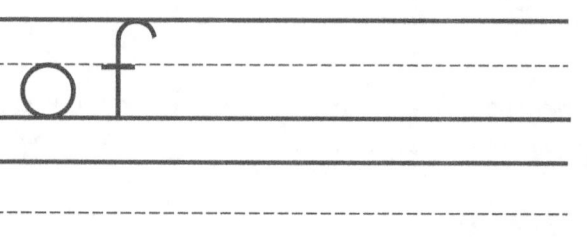

Spell
Circle the correct spelling of the word.

of   ov   off   of

Trace the word 'of' to complete the sentence. Read the sentence.

Dan is in a den of big cats.

Color the word. Then write it in your word bank book.

Name _____   Date _____

 High Frequency Word

Read
Say the word.

Write
Write the word.

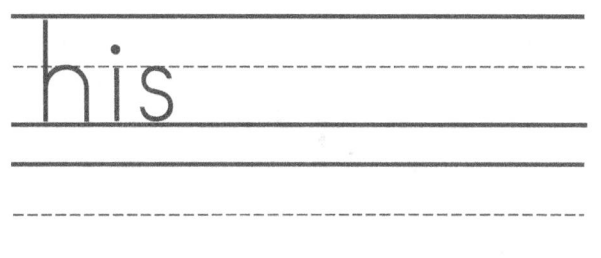

Spell
Circle the correct spelling of the word.

is   his   has   his

Trace the word 'his' to complete the sentence. Read the sentence.

Ron hid his bag of nuts.

Color the word. Then write it in your word bank book.

© Quail Publishers LLC 2023   Bible Phonics Workbook 2 | 27

Name _____   Date _____

 High Frequency Word

Read
Say the word.

has

Write
Write the word.

has

Spell
Circle the correct spelling of the word.

as   has   his   has

Trace the word '**has**' to complete the sentence. Read the sentence.

Ben has a big sack on his back.

Color the word. Then write it in your word bank book.

The /l/ Sound

Say the picture name. Listen for the **first** sound. Say the sound.

lion

Story Time: Listen carefully as your teacher, or parent, reads the Bible story below. What did you learn from the story?

Bible Story: Daniel in the Lions' Den
Bible Lesson: Daniel 6:1-28
Bible Theme: Do What is Right

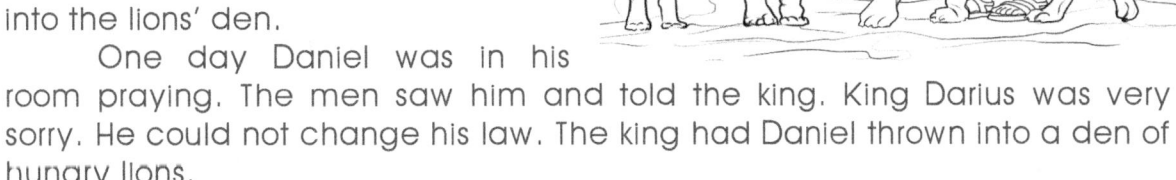

King Darius loved Daniel very much and made him his chief advisor. Some men heard about it and got very jealous. They tricked the king into passing a bad law. The law said that no one should worship any god for thirty days unless it was the king. If anyone did, they would be thrown into the lions' den.

One day Daniel was in his room praying. The men saw him and told the king. King Darius was very sorry. He could not change his law. The king had Daniel thrown into a den of hungry lions.

"Daniel may your god save you," King Darius said.

That night the king could not eat or sleep. Early the next morning, he rushed to the lions' den. He called out to Daniel.

Daniel said, "May the king live forever! God sent his angel to shut the lions' mouths. They did not hurt me, for I have done no wrong." The king was happy. He threw the wicked men into the lions' den.

King Darius told everyone that the "God of Daniel lives forever. He protects. He saves." **God saves us when we do what is right.**

Name _____ Date _____

Handwriting
Trace and write.

Spelling
Say the name of each picture. Then write the missing letters to complete the words.

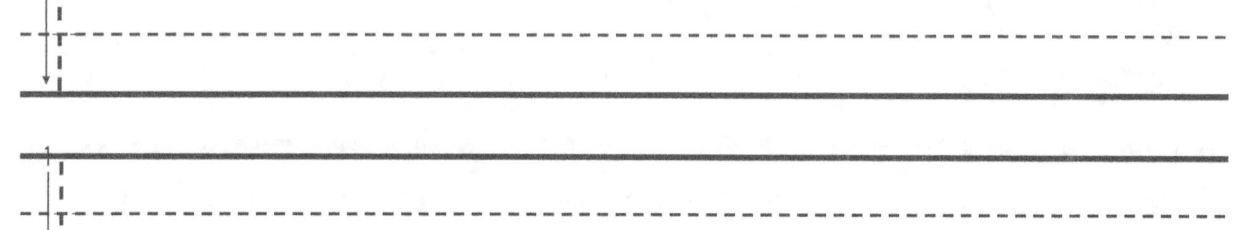

___adder   wa___rus   came___

Identifying Sounds
Say the name of each picture. Then circle those that **begin** with the sound /l/.

Name _____   Date _____

The /l/ Sound

Say the picture name. Listen for the <u>last</u> sound. Say the sound. The letters 'll' stand for one sound, /l/ as in hill.

hill

Phonics Tip: When the sound /l/ is heard after a short vowel sound in a one-syllable word, it is usually spelled with the letters 'll'. For example: hill.

Blending

Use sound talk to say the letter sounds in each word. Then blend the sounds to read the words. How many sounds are in each word?

Reading

Read the sentence based on Exodus 24:12-14.

The man is on top of the hill.

Name _____ Date _____

The /s/ Sound

Say the picture name. Listen for the <u>last</u> sound. Say the sound. The letters '**ss**' stand for one sound, /**s**/ as in cro**ss**.

  cro**ss**

Phonics Tip: When the sound /**s**/ is heard after a short vowel sound in a one-syllable word, it is usually spelled with the letters '**ss**'. For example: cro**ss**.

Blending

Use sound talk to say the letter sounds in each word. Then blend the sounds to read the words. How many sounds are in each word?

miss   toss   fuss

kiss   mass   less

Reading

Read the sentence based on Luke 23:33.

The man of God is on a cross.

32   © Quail Publishers LLC 2023   Bible Phonics Workbook 2

Name _____ Date _____

Blending
Use sound talk to say the letter sounds in each word. Then blend the sounds to read the words.

f u n   l e g   b u t

l e t   m i ss   t e ll

Spelling
Say the picture names. Then circle the correct spelling for each picture.

fan fin   leg log   bug bag

Reading
Read the sentence.

Ben and Lin run in the hot sun.

Name _____ Date _____

High Frequency Word

Read
Say the word.

go

Write
Write the word.

go

Spell
Circle the correct spelling of the word.

go   so   go   got

Trace the word 'go' to complete the sentence. Read the sentence.

The men go up the hill.

Color the word. Then write it in your word bank book.

go

Name _____ Date _____

High Frequency Word

Read
Say the word.

no

Write
Write the word.

no

Spell
Circle the correct spelling of the word.

n o   s o   g o   n o

Trace the word 'no' to complete the sentences. Read the sentences.

No lid is on the pot.

Ted has no pen.

Color the word. Then write it in your word bank book.

no

Name _____   Date _____

High Frequency Word

Read
Say the word.

so

Write
Write the word.

so

Spell
Circle the correct spelling of the word.

go   so   no   so

Trace the word '**so**' to complete the sentences. Read the sentences.

The sun is so hot.

The bed is so big.

Color the word. Then write it in your word bank book.

so

Name _____   Date _____

Reviewing Sounds

Beginning Sounds: Say the name of each picture. Listen carefully for the <u>first</u> sound. Circle the letter that stands for the sound.

r   h   l

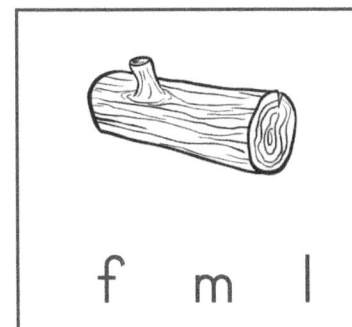
f   m   l

v   f   s

Middle Sounds: Say the name of each picture. Listen carefully for the <u>middle</u> sound. Circle the letter that stands for the sound.

o   u   e

e   i   o

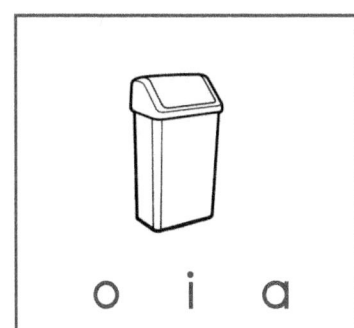
o   i   a

End Sounds: Say the name of each picture. Listen carefully for the <u>last</u> sound. Circle the letter that stands for the sound.

r   f   l

b   t   p

l   b   g

Name _____   Date _____

Rhymes
Connect the Rhymes: Read the words below. Draw a line to connect those that rhyme.

hen   rug
hill   luck
bug   bill
cap   pen
duck   gap

Find the rhymes: Write the word from the box that rhymes with each underlined word to complete the captions.

| sun   mug   hill |
| hat   puff |

A <u>bug</u> in a _____.

<u>Run</u> in the _____.

A <u>cat</u> in a _____.

A <u>mill</u> on a _____.

<u>Huff</u> and _____.

Name _____   Date _____

Word Building with Vowels: Add vowels to complete the words. Read the new words you made. Use them in sentences.

Add 'u'	Add 'e'	Add 'a'
c__p	b__ll	h__t
m__d	p__ck	l__b
h__g	b__d	r__g
p__ff	h__n	m__ss

Word Families: Read the words. Then place them under the correct word family.

bell   nut   rug   sell
bug   hut   but   fell   hug

-ut word	-ug words	-ell words
_____	_____	_____
_____	_____	_____
_____	_____	_____

Name _____   Date _____

Steps to Spelling

- **Look** carefully at each picture.
- **Say** the picture name.
- **Listen** for the letter sounds.
- **Write** the letters that represent the sounds. Use the sound buttons (•) to guide you. Each stands for **one** sound. A sound button below a long line (──•──) represents a digraph (two letters that stand for one sound).
- **Read** the words that you have written.
- **Check** your spelling.

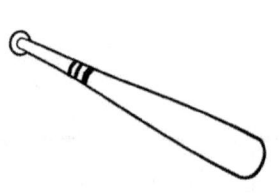
___ ___ ___
 •   •   •

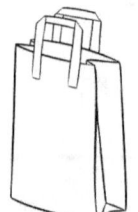
___ ___ ___
 •   •   •

___ ___ ___ ___
 •   •   •   •

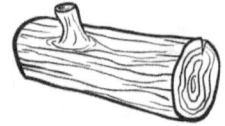
___ ___ ___
 •   •   •

___ ___ ___
 •   •   •

___ ___ ___
 •   •   •

Guess the Riddles: Listen carefully as your teacher, or parent, reads the riddles below. Then write the missing letters to complete the word.

It gives light during the day.   s ___ ___

A female fowl or bird.   h ___ ___

You use it to bathe.   r ___ ___

You sleep on it.   b ___ ___

Name _____   Date _____

The Alphabet
Every letter has a position in the alphabet. Write the missing letters of the alphabet in their upper and lowercase forms.

Aa	____	Cc	Dd
____	Ff	____	____	Ii
Jj	Kk	____	Mm	Nn
Oo	Pp	Qq	____	Ss
Tt	____	Vv	Ww	Xx
Yy	Zz

Letter Shapes
Match each uppercase letter with its lowercase form.

E   h   B   f

U   e   F   l

R   u   L   b

H   r

Bible Phonics Workbook 2 | 41

Name _____   Date _____

Picture Clues
Use the pictures as clues to help you to spell the missing words and complete the sentences. Read the sentences.

1. The men ran in the hot _____ .

2. Dan got off the _____ .

3. The fog hid the _____ hut.

4. No _____ is in the bag.

5. The sick man is in his _____ .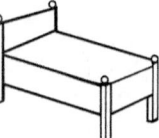

6. The _____ hid the cat.

7. Ben fed the hen and _____ .

8. A big cod is in the _____ .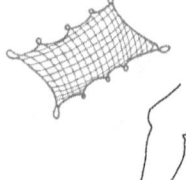

9. The bad dog bit Dad on his _____ .

10. A _____ is on the cot.

Name _____ Date _____

Comprehension: Read the passage below and answer the questions.

Pam's Backpack

It is Pam.

Pam has a backpack.

It is a big backpack.

A rag is in the backpack.

A pen is in the backpack.

A hat is in the backpack.

Pam gets in a big bus.

And the bus is off.

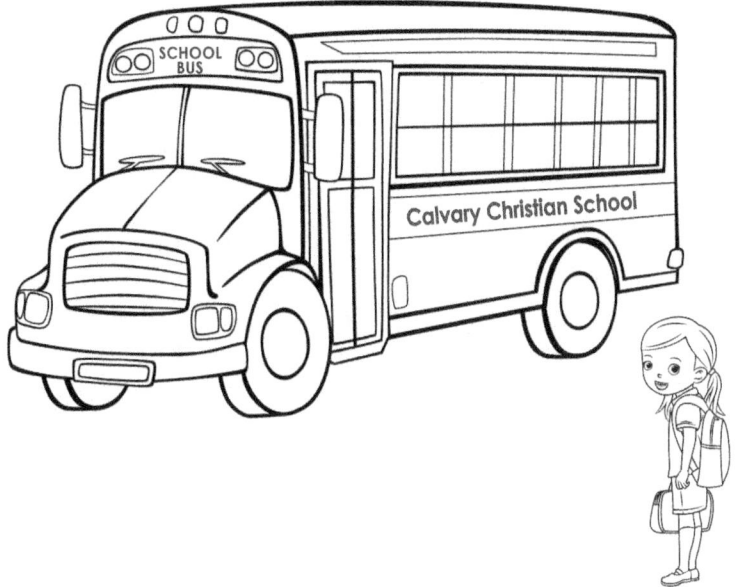

Write the correct word on the line to complete each sentence.

1. Pam has a _____.
   a. sack   b. backpack   d. pack

2. Pam gets in a _____.
   a. cab   b. bus   c. rag

3. Pam has a _____ in the backpack.
   a. tablet   b. bus   c. rag

Discussion
1. Name some other things that Pam **may** have in her backpack. Name some things you have in your backpack.
2. Where do you think Pam is going?
3. Is Pam's school different from other schools? If so, why?

Name _____ Date _____

Building Sentences: Read the sentence based on Luke 15:11-32.

A sad man is in the pigpen.

Write a sentence about the picture. Make sure that you follow your checklist.

Capital Letter	Spelling	Handwriting	Finger spaces	Punctuation	Sentence Makes Sense
A	sat	✋	☝	•	😐

Reading: Read the following sentences.

Ned got off the bus at ten.

Mom locks up the pigpen.

The sun is so hot.

Rob hid the map in the hut.

The doll is on a cot.

Ten sick men met a man of God.

The fog hid the sun.

A big rat hid in the sack.

Kim had bun and ham.

The hens peck the sack of nuts.

The pup fell in the mud.

Bill has a big sack on his back.

Syllables. Some words have two parts. Each part has one vowel sound.

1. Blend the sounds to read the first part of the word.
2. Then blend the sounds to read the second part of the word.
3. Put the two parts together to read the word.

lap / top = laptop
tab / let = tablet
pig / let = piglet
sun / set = sunset
in / to = into
up / set = upset
up / on = upon
un / til = until
muf / fin = muffin
rib / bon = ribbon
Lon / don = London

Colors and their Names. These are some colors and their names that you must learn. Name some objects in the Bible with these colors.

Read it Say the words.	Write it Trace the words.	Spell it Write the words.	Color it Color the objects.
red	red		
blue	blue		
yellow	yellow		
green	green		
orange	orange		
brown	brown		
purple	purple		
black	black		
white	white		

Word List:

Below is a list of words with the letters and sounds taught in this workbook. The list also includes high frequency words. Read the words, then use them to build sentences.

Letter Sets	Words			
8 e u r h	**+ e**	**+ u**	**+ r**	**+ h**
High Frequency met up us had ten him hid *the *to	set pet net met get ten pen den men neck peck peg	up us sun nun sup cup mud mum gum mug tug suck tuck muck duck	rat rap ram rag rig rip rim run rum rug rot rock Rick red	had hat ham hid hit him hip hog hop hen hut hug hock heck hack
9 b f ff l	**+ b**	**+ f**	**+ff**	**+ l**
High Frequency but back big if let off *of *his *has	bat ban bag bad back big bit beg bed bus bug bun bud back sob mob tab tub hub buck	fan fat fit fin fig fog fed fun if	off cuff huff puff	lap lad lag lit lip lot log let leg lick lack lock luck
10 ll ss	**+ ll**	**+ ss**		
High Frequency no* go* so* tell	ill sill pill dill mill gill fill kill Bill doll sell tell bell hell fell gull dull	ass mass miss kiss hiss less mess toss moss Tess fuss		
	Simple words with two syllables			
	sun/set = sunset			
	back/pack = backpack			
	mel/on = melon			
	lem/on = lemon			
	pal/let = pallet			

www.ingramcontent.com/pod-product-compliance
Lightning Source LLC
Chambersburg PA
CBHW082248300426
44110CB00039B/2478